3 excuses to give up learning Welsh

A learner's guide to some bothersome Welsh grammar

Jack Pulman-Slater

Llundain 2019

Jack Pulman-Slater: *3 excuses to give up learning Welsh*

© Jack Pulman-Slater, 2019
All rights reserved

www.jackpulmanslater.com

Cover illustration: Lucy Culshaw

ISBN: 978-0-244-46253-6

Contents

Introduction 4
How to use this book 6
Excuse #1: the mutations 8
   Rules to get it right every time 10
   The Soft Mutation 13
      What causes a soft mutation? 14
   The Nasal Mutation 18
      What causes a nasal mutation? 19
   The Aspirate Mutation 22
      What causes an aspirate mutation? 22
   "Cryptogenic mutations" 24
   The mutations: Be' sy'n bod? 28
Excuse #2: Saying 'yes' and 'no' 30
   Present tense questions with *to be* 32
      What about **oes**? 34
   Past tense with *to be* 36
   Past tense without *to be* 38
   Future tense with *to be* 40
   Conditional tense with *to be* 42
   Cael: *to have/get* 43
   Gwneud: *to do/make* 45
   Emphatic questions 46
   Yes/No: Be' sy'n bod? 48
Excuse #3: the verb *to be* 49
   First person: *I* 51
   First person plural: *we* 53
   Second person: *you* 54
   Third person: *he/she, they* 55
      What about **yw**? 57
   Sydd yn/sy'n 59
   Negatives 60
      First person: *I* 62
      Second person: *you* 63

    Third person: *he/she, they* 64
    Sa, so, so, so, so, so 64
  What about *bu*? 65
  The verb *to be*: Be' sy'n bod? 68
Grammatical Glossary 69
Answers: Be' sy'n bod? 86
  The mutations 86
  Yes/No 88
  The verb *to be* 89
Gair o ddiolch 90

Introduction

Whenever someone from outside Wales learns that I am a Welsh speaker and teacher they always ask whether Welsh is "similar to English". If you are an adult learner of the language you will know that the answer is "no" (or perhaps "are you joking?"). In Welsh, you can't say you "have a turtle" you have to say that one is "with" you or "by" you. Until you've made a bit of progress, a dictionary is completely useless for looking up the meaning of Welsh words because the first letters of most words beginning with consonants change into other letters depending on... never mind, we'll deal with this one later. Perhaps the most frustratingly mind-baffling feature of the language for beginners is the fact that there isn't just one single pair of words corresponding to "yes" and "no".

If you only speak one language it can be difficult to understand and appreciate that the way your language carves up the world linguistically is just one way that human language can manifest itself. The idea that a language might put words in a different order, or lack a word your language has, or need several words for a concept your language describes with just a single word can cause a headache. Lots of people who come to adult second language classes don't feel they have the skills and linguistic insight they need to feel comfortable with how another language works. The types of linguistic insecurities learners tell me about in class are made worse by overly complicated grammar books filled with technical grammatical terms learners don't understand ("what even is the pluperfect tense!? Does it exist in English?"). Another thing that exacerbates linguistic insecurity is the use of apps, podcasts and language learning material that just encourage learners to repeat things. Learning stock phrases means you can respond reasonably well when you're down the pub and someone who finds out you're learning Welsh says "go on then, say something in Welsh!". But this kind of mindless rote-learning isn't linguistic. Humans are good at language, you have a lot of intuitive grammatical knowledge even if you only speak one language and learning a second language should let you tap into this linguistic potential. I hope this book will enable you to do more than "say something in Welsh"- I hope you'll be able to say something of Welsh and gain some grammatical insight that will help you on your way to becoming an increasingly confident Welsh speaker and reader.

This book is for adult learners of the Welsh language. We're going to look at three linguistic eccentricities of Welsh- these three things are hallmarks of the Welsh language that could be used as legitimate excuses for packing in the whole language learning endeavour altogether. The three grammatical characteristics we will consider are the things learners tell me they'll never get their heads around because they just make Welsh so different to English. We're going to clear the muddied Cymric waters. You don't need to be a grammarian or a polyglot to read this book. You don't need to know what the imperfect subjunctive is. You don't need to have a degree in Linguistics. You've got everything you need already: an interest in Welsh, a brain and this book.

How to use this book

Yn y bôn the important underlying concepts are in these sections. Get your head around this stuff before you read on.

Yn Saesneg some sections start with a list of sentences in English that will let you know what the section will help you say in Welsh.

Er enghraifft examples of the sentence patterns or grammatical rules discussed in a particular section of the book.

Watcha mas! Watch out and avoid the traps or common mistakes by checking these sections.

Diolch byth! Keep positive by reading the good news sections which draw attention to simple exceptions to complex stuff.

Be' sy'n bod? Use what you've just demystified straight away by trying these quick exercises. There's one error in each sentence- correct it. Answers are at the back.

Mae brawddegau a geiriau Cymraeg mewn llythrennau bras ac mae cyfieithiadau yn Saesneg mewn llythrennau italig.
Welsh words and sentences are in bold and translations in English are in italics.

Weithiau mae brawddeg yn Gymraeg gyda chyfieithiad i'r Saesneg ac wedyn cyfieithiad llythrennol mewn tabl:

Sometimes there is a sentence in Welsh with a translation in English, followed by a literal translation in a table:

Weithiau	mae	brawddeg	yn	Gymraeg	gyda	chyfieithiad
Sometimes	*is*	*sentence*	PARTICLE	Welsh	with	translation

Grammatical terms are underlined. Head to the Grammatical Glossary at the back for accessible definitions with clear Welsh and English examples.

Voiceless lateral fricative[1]

*Sentences what have an asterisk by them is grammatically incorrect

---

[1] Geeky phonetic terms are in footnotes. These are the scientific names for describing the sounds of the language. A quick internet search of these terms will give you a recording of the sound. Don't worry about these terms, unless you're of a phonetic persuasion!

Excuse #1: the mutations

"I feel I will die of mutations"
Beginner level learner

In his book 'Lingo', Gaston Dorren[2] observes that the mutation system of Welsh '[...] makes life hell for second language learners while being riddled with rules that can seem to be all but pointless'. When the adult learner is introduced to the mutations for the first time, this sounds like a fair assessment. It seems bonkers.

A dictionary isn't much use for Welsh unless you have made some progress with the mutations system. If I tell you that my **mrawd** lives in London, you wouldn't be able to find this word in the dictionary. This word could also crop up as **frawd**, but in order to find the correct meaning you'd have to look up the word **brawd**. The mutations system means that the word for *Wales* could be spelt **Nghymru** if I'm talking about something in the country or **Gymru** if I'm travelling over the Severn Bridge or **Chymru** if I'm listing a lot of countries and the Land of my Fathers is the last item on the list. It's my **nhractor**, but her **thractor** and his **dractor**. I've got a **cath ddu**, however, my dog is the same colour, but it's a **ci du** not a **ci ddu**. Off to the rugby? Remember, it's **sospan fach**, but the cat has scratched **Johnny bach**, not **Johnny fach**.

Whilst this may seem absurd, mutations do matter. They let us know whether a sentence is positive or negative, signal possession as well as give us possible clues about case. In short, we need mutations to signal grammatical distinctions. You won't die of mutations because you mutate words every day- you just don't know it yet. The idea of the first letters of words changing depending on where they appear in a sentence isn't completely alien- it happens in English.

Say the following sentences at a reasonable conversational speed:

---

[2] Dorren, G., 2015. *Lingo: Around Europe in Sixty Languages*. Grove/Atlantic, Inc..

1) I live in Cardiff

2) I live in Budapest

When we say these sentences in continuous speech, we almost certainly say the word *in* differently depending on the following word. For example, when we say sentence 1, unless we are enunciating each word carefully, we don't say "in", but instead say something like "*I live ing Cardiff*"[3]. In sentence 2, the *n* of the word *in* probably ends up sounds like "im" and the word *Budapest* probably sounds like it starts with an *m*: "*im mudapest*"[4]. In other words, the mouth changes sounds by adjusting to the articulation of the previous and upcoming sounds. Linguists call this phenomenon coarticulation. It's something that happens in all spoken languages in the world. Lots of the mutations in Welsh involve this kind of natural sound change motivated by how sounds change in connected speech.

The mutations system in Welsh involves changing one sound for another at the start of words. Above we looked at how sounds can change into others when influenced by adjacent sounds. However, lots of mutations aren't caused in this way- sometimes a sound will change into another one because there is a fundamental link between them. We can see this happening in other languages as well as in certain dialects of English. If you know some Spanish or have ever tried to pronounce some Spanish words, then you might have noticed that sounds which are distinct in English are blurred together in Spanish. Words beginning with **b** are often pronounced with a **v**[5] sound instead, e.g. **vevo** (*I live*) often sounds like "*bebo*". The same blurring effect happens with **d** and **th** sounds, e.g. **a la derecha** (*on the right*) often sounds like "a la therecha". The fact that languages can swap between sounds like this tells us something about the properties of the sounds being swapped: they are phonetically similar. **b** and **v** are pronounced in very similar places in the mouth; they are also both voiced sounds (i.e. produced with a buzz in the voice box- don't worry, we'll look at this

---

[3] We could write this using the International Phonetic Alphabet as /aɪ lɪv ɪŋ kɑːdɪf/ instead of /ɪn kɑːdɪf/

[4] /aɪ lɪv ɪm mʊdəpest/ versus /ɪn mʊdəpest/

[5] For those interested in this kind of thing, the phonetic symbol is /β/ (a voiced bilabial fricative)

idea in more detail later). Spaniards can swap a **th**-type sound for a **d**-type sound because these sounds share certain properties- they're almost the same sound. Think about how lots of people in England pronounce the **th** sound as **f** or **v**, e.g. "*I fink so*". **th** sounds and **f** sounds are extremely similar: they are both voiceless fricative sounds (i.e. quiet sounds with no voice box buzz and pronounced with scratchy turbulence in the mouth) made towards the front of the mouth. It's no accident that **f** creeps in to replace **th** sounds.

These are really the kind of sound changes we're talking about with Welsh- it's not that bonkers at all really. These kinds of changes happen naturally in all languages, it's just that some languages like to record more accurately in writing what's happening in the mouth when its speakers speak. In Welsh, these natural tendencies to adjust sounds as we speak have become fossilized in the language and now make important grammatical distinctions. The key to understanding the mutations is to stop thinking about letters (i.e. A, B, C, D etc.) and to start thinking about sounds instead. Think nursery school alphabet ah, buh, cuh, duh and not A, B, C, D. Think about the sounds the letters represent instead of the English names for the letters. It's sounds and how they are pronounced that we'll consider in the next section.

Rules to get it right every time

Yn y bôn

- The first consonant of a word changes and is replaced wholesale with a new sound
- The changes are restricted and rule-driven- it's not a free-for-all
- The changes are natural and motivated by how our mouths make the sounds
- There are three types of mutation: soft, nasal and aspirate

At first, it can seem like the mutations system is random. However, there are a few underlying rules, which if learned, will mean you will always be able to select the correct mutation:

Rule 1: When mutating a sound, the place of articulation almost always remains the same (or very near) across the series. E.g. **p** is mutated softly, nasally and aspirately under a variety of grammatical conditions, however, **p** can only mutate into a sound that is articulated with both the lips pressed together[6]. The same principle applies to **c**: below is a cross-section of the mouth and throat with the place of articulation for all the mutations of **c**.

Place of articulation for all mutations of c

g is simply a voiced variant of **c** (just like the difference in English between *cap* and *gap*), and the nasal sound **ngh** simply a nasal version of **c**. All these sounds are made at the back of the tongue[7], so we're making three different sounds in one place in our mouth. This is efficient and also really quite nifty when you think about it.

Rule 2: In the nasal and aspirate mutations, the initial voicing distinction of the original sound is retained. For example, **p** is a voiceless sound (i.e. you don't vibrate your voice box to make the sound **p**- it's quiet) and mutates nasally to the voiceless nasal sound **mh**, whilst **b** is a voiced sound and mutates nasally to the voiced sound **m**.

---

[6] bilabial sounds
[7] velar sounds

If you put your fingers over your neck where your voice box is (don't strangle yourself, a light touch will do!) you can feel the difference between sounds we're calling voiced and ones we're calling voiceless. Try saying **b** and then **p**. You should be able to feel that when you say **b** you can feel a vibration in your throat that you can't feel when you say **p**. Remember we're talking about the sounds **b** and **p** and not the names for these letters, i.e. we're talking about "buh" and "puh" not "Bee" and "Pee". Try saying some words in English beginning with **b** in English and contrast them with words beginning with **p** to make sure you're clear on the distinction between voiced and voiceless sounds. Understanding the difference between voiced and voiceless sounds will help you learn the mutations with insight.

Rule 3: There is a restricted set of possibilities, e.g. the aspirate sounds are all voiceless fricative sounds (i.e. quiet and scratchy sounds). Sometimes it's impossible to have a mutated version of a sound, e.g. there is no nasal version of **rh** or **ll** (what would this sound like?). Likewise, **m** doesn't mutate nasally because it's already a nasal sound.

The Soft Mutation

P	B	**partner > ei bartner**
		partner > his partner
T	D	**tad > ei dad**
		dad > his dad
C	G	**cath > ei gath**
		cat > his cat
B	F	**brawd > ei frawd**
		brother > his brother
D	Dd	**desg > ei ddesg**
		desk > his desk
G	-	**gwely > ei wely**
		bed > his bed
Ll	L	**llyfr > ei lyfr**
		book > his book
M	F	**mam > ei fam**
		mum > his mum
Rh	R	**rhaff > ei raff**
		rope > his rope

Think about the sound changes in the table above. We need to spot the patterns we spoke about in the previous section in order to confidently and correctly mutate. As you read the examples and explanations of the mutations, make sure you say the sounds out loud and think about how the way you make each sound in the pair is fundamentally similar. Remember, the key to getting this right is understanding the sounds the letters represent.

The soft mutation involves making sounds louder, thicker or more prominent, either by voicing an unvoiced sound (e.g. **c** > **g**) or by making a sound fricative (i.e. scratchy) (e.g. **d** > **dd**).

Below are the consonants which involve a change in voicing (i.e. from no buzz in the voice box to a buzz. Or put it another way: from quiet to loud):

p > b

t > d

c > g

The rest of the soft mutation series involves slightly different changes. The changes below all involve making a sounds fricative (i.e. scratchy) and, in so doing, changing the place of articulation every-so-slightly.

b > f

d > dd

m > f

The remaining three sound changes in slightly different ways.

- **ll > l** this is the change from a scratchy voiceless sound[8] to a voiced sound (i.e. with a voice box buzz).
- **rh > r** this is the change from a voiceless trilled **r** to a voiced trilled **r**[9].
- **g** is an exception and doesn't involve a sound change at all- it simply disappears.

What causes a soft mutation?

The following list isn't at all exhaustive; however, it does include the most common situations where you will need a soft mutation conversationally. There are unfortunately, but necessarily, lots of grammatical terms in this section. But remember to head to the Grammatical Glossary at the back of the book for explanations and examples of underlined terms.

The soft mutation occurs to all sounds in the series except **rh** and **ll** under the following conditions:

---

[8] Using technical phonetic terms we would say the change is from a voiceless lateral fricative /ɬ/ to a voiced lateral approximant /l/ (i.e. a "normal" English **L**-sound).
[9] Those of Phonetic persuasion would call this the change from a voiceless alveolar trill to a voiced alveolar trill.

➤ Singular feminine nouns with the definite article or the number **un** (*one*)

- **y + cath > y gath** (*the cat*)

➤ Nouns or adjectives used predicatively or adverbially after **yn**

- **Mae e'n + Cymro > Mae e'n Gymro** (*He is a Welshman*)
- **Mae e'n + deallus > Mae e'n ddeallus** (*He is clever*)
- **Cerddodd hi'n + cylfym > cerddodd hi'n gyflym** (*She walked quickly*)

➤ Adjectives following **mor** (*so*) or **rhy** (*too*)

- **Mae e mor + tawel > Mae e mor dawel** (*He is so quiet*)
- **Roedd e'n rhy + drud > roedd e'n rhy ddrud** (*It was too expensive*)

Common situations where the full soft mutation occurs (i.e. including **Rh** and **Ll**):

➤ Adjectives, nouns or verbal-nouns used to qualify singular feminine nouns

- **cath + bach > cath fach** ([a] *small cat*)
- **athrawes + mathemateg > athrawes fathemateg** ([a] *maths teacher*)

➤ Words immediately following the prepositions **am** (*for*), **ar** (*on*), **at** (*at*), **dan** (*under*), **dros** (*over*), **trwy** (*through*), **heb** (*without*), **hyd** (*until*), **gan** (*by*), **wrth** (*from*), **i** (*to*), **o** (*of*)

- **Aeth e i + Llanelli > Aeth i Lanelli** (*He went to Llanelli*)
- **O + Caerydd mae e'n dod yn wreiddiol > O Gaerdydd mae e'n dod yn wreiddiol** (*He's originally from Cardiff*)

- **Ces i hwn wrth + cyngor y dref > Ces i hwn wrth gyngor y dref** (*I got this from the town council*)

➧ Nouns following the numbers *dau / dwy* (*two*)

- **dau + ci > dau gi** (*two dogs*)
- **dwy + cath > dwy gath** (*two cats*)

➧ Nouns following adjectives (n.b. most adjectives follow the noun);

- **hen + brithyll > hen frithyll** ([*an*] *old trout*)

➧ Nouns after the possessive pronouns **dy** (*your*[10]) and **ei** (*his*).

- **dy + partner > dy bartner** (*your partner*)
- **ei + car > ei gar** (*his car*)

➧ Direct objects which appear straight after the subject

- **Gwelodd e + blaidd > Gwelodd e flaidd** (*He saw a wolf*)

➧ Infinitives which appear straight after an indirect object

- **Rhaid i fi + mynd > Rhaid i fi fynd** (*I have to go*)

---

[10] [informal/singular]

➤ The second element in lots of <u>compound words</u>

- **Llan** + **Mair** > **Llanfair** *(the Parish of St Mary's)*

➤ <u>Interrogative</u> <u>short-form</u> <u>verbs</u> in the past <u>tense</u>.

- **Cest ti amser** *(You had time)* > **Gest ti amser?** *(Did you have time?)*
- **Daeth e i'r parti** *(He came to the party)* > **Ddaeth e i'r parti?** *(Did he come to the party?)*

➤ <u>Negative</u> <u>short-form</u> verbs beginning with **b, d, g, ll, m, rh**[11]

- **Brathodd y ci y ficer** *(The dog bit the vicar)* > **Frathodd y ci mo'r ficar** *(The dog didn't bite the vicar)*
- **Dywedais i wrthi hi** *(I told her)* > **Ddywedais i ddim wrthi hi** *(I didn't tell her)*
- **Gwelais i'r rhaglen** *(I saw the programme)* > **Welais mo'r rhaglen** *(I didn't see the programme)*

---

[11] Lots of varieties of Welsh softly mutate all negative short-form verbs. The rule here is the situation in "standard" Welsh- whatever "standard Welsh" is…

The Nasal Mutation

P	Mh	**partner > fy mhartner** *partner > my partner*
T	Nh	**tad > fy nhad** *dad > my dad*
C	Ngh	**cath > fy nghath** *cat > my cat*
B	M	**brawd > fy mrawd** *brother > my brother*
D	N	**desg > fy nesg** *desk > my desk*
G	Ng	**gwely > fy ngwely** *bed > my bed*

The nasal mutations only happen to a subset of the consonants that can take a mutation. It's a sound change that involves taking a consonant and turning it into a nasal sound. Nasal sounds are made by air flowing through the nose, e.g. in the word *singing* there are two nasal sounds represented by the letters **ng**. This **ng** sound is made by bunching the back of your tongue up against the back of the roof of your mouth and blowing air out through your nose whilst vibrating your voice box.

In Welsh, there are voiced and voiceless nasals. Voiceless nasals are quite rare in the languages of the world. In Europe, it's really only Wales and Iceland that have these voiceless nasal sounds. I love a good voiceless nasal- they're part of the unique linguistic heritage of Welsh. Let's make sure we get these sorted, so on your next trip to Iceland you can stand in Þingvellir, the Aurora Borialis above you, and feel a Celtic-Norse connection[12].

---

[12] It's so windy in Iceland though- wonder how they actually hear all these beautiful, quiet, nasal whisperings…

Voiceless nasal sounds involve air flowing out of the nose, but with no voice box buzz (i.e. no vibrating of the larynx). The sounds in the voiceless table below are all really just made by breathing out through the nose by making blockages at different locations in the mouth. For **mh** you make a blockage at the lips, for **nh** you make the blockage behind your teeth and for **ngh** you make the blockage in the same part of your mouth as you do twice in the word *singing*.

Unmutated voiceless consonants	Voiceless nasals
P	Mh
T	Nh
C	Ngh

Unmutated voiced consonants	Voiced nasal
B	M
D	N
G	Ng

What causes a nasal mutation?

Diolch byth!

The short answer is "not a lot". Only two words cause nasal mutations.

➻ Nouns and verbal-nouns following **fy** (*my*)

- **fy + car > fy nghar** (*my car*)

- **Rwyt ti'n fy + casáu > fy nghasáu** (*You hate me*)

➤ Nouns following the particle **yn** (*in*)

- **Dw i'n byw yn + Caerdydd > Dw i'n byw yng Nghaerdydd** (*I live in Cardiff*
- **Arhoson ni yn + Trefdraeth > Arhoson ni yn Nhrefdraeth** (*We stayed in Newport[13]*)
- **Mae'r bocs yn + gwaelod y cwpwrdd > Mae'r bocs yng ngwaelod y cwpwrdd** (*The box is in the back of the cupboard*)

1| Watcha mas!

Yn can mean two different things and each separate meaning causes a different kind of mutation.

When **yn** appears before a verb or an adjective, it's serving as a present tense particle, e.g.

1. **Dw i'n canu** (*I'm singing*)
2. **Dw i'n grac** (*I'm angry*)

In both sentences **yn** doesn't mean *in*, it's just appearing before something being described: an action underway (in sentence 1) and an emotional state (in sentence 2). In grammatical terms, it's introducing the predicate. **Yn** before adjectives causes a soft mutation, e.g. **yn + crac > yn grac**. However, **yn** before a verb doesn't cause a mutation.

When **yn** appears before a noun or a location (i.e. something that something else can physically be inside of) it's being used as a preposition- it's giving us information about the relationship between two objects or places. **Yn** in these contexts causes a nasal mutation:

---

[13] Newport, Pembrokeshire ("West is Best!")

- **Maen nhw'n byw ym Mhortiwgal** (*They live in Portugal*)
    - Yn + Portiwgal
- **Mae'r farchnad yng nghanol y dref** (*the market's in the town centre*)
    - Yn + canol
- **Ym mwrlwm y ddinas** (*in the hubbub of the city*)
    - yn + bwrlwm

2 | Watcha mas!

When using **yn** to mean *in*, not only does the following <u>noun</u> need to change, but also the form of **yn** itself. Notice that they have to match in terms of place of articulation, i.e. the end of the words **yn** blends with the beginning of the following word.

- **ym**
    - yn + Porth > ym Mhorth
    - yn + Borth > ym Morth
- **yn**
    - yn + Trefdraeth > yn Nhrefdraeth
    - yn + Dolwen > yn Nolwen
- **yng**
    - yn + Caerdydd > yng Nghaerdydd
    - yn + Gwent > yng Ngwent

The Aspirate Mutation

P	Ph	partner > ei phartner
		partner > her partner
T	Ch	tad > ei thad
		dad > her dad
C	Ch	cath > ei chath
		cat > her cat

The aspirate mutation happens to an even more restricted set of consonants than the nasal mutation. Keep thinking about sounds and not letters. When you look through the table above, try and think about how the unmutated and the mutated sounds are similar. Both **c** and **ch** are pronounced in the same place in the mouth (at the back where you'd make the sound at the end of the word *sing*). Aspirate sounds are always voiceless (i.e. quiet sounds) and they're always fricative (i.e. scratchy). So when you're thinking about aspirate mutations you need to match the place of articulation and make sure you're mutating a quiet sound into another quiet sound. It's not a free-for-all. You can't go from **p** (a quiet sound made with both the lips) to **nh** because this wouldn't keep the place of articulation the same (**nh** is made by blocking the airflow behind the teeth). Likewise, you couldn't go from a word beginning with **b** and mutate it into **mh** because **b** is a voiced sound and **mh** is a voiceless sound. Remember: aspirate mutations have to keep the original sound's place of articulation (i.e. where it's made in the mouth) and retain the voiceless/quiet property of the sound.

What causes an aspirate mutation?

➨ The <u>possessive pronoun</u> **ei** (*her*), also **i'w** (*to her*) and **a'i** (*and her*)

- **ei + tractor > ei thractor** (*her tractor*)
- **i'w + tŷ > i'w thŷ** (*to her house*)
- **a'i + plant > a'i phlant** (and *her children*)

- **Does neb wedi dod yma i'w + clywed > chlywed** (*No-one's come here to hear her*)

➤ The numerals **tri** (*three,* masculine) and **chwe** (*six*):

- **tri + tŷ > tri thŷ** (*three houses*)
- **chwe + cadair > chwe chadair** (*six chairs*)

➤ The <u>adverb</u> **tra** (*very*)

- **nofel tra + pwysig > nofel tra phwysig** (*a very powerful novel*)

➤ After the <u>conjunctions</u> **a** (*and*), **â** (*with, as*), **na** (*nor, than*)

- **pen a papur > pen a phapur** (*pen and paper*)
- **Mae e'n siarad â + pobl > Mae e'n siarad â phobl** (*He's talking to people*)
- **Mae'n waeth na + cael gwaith i'w wneud ar y penwythnos > Mae'n waeth na chael gwaith i'w wneud ar y penwythnos** (*It's worse than having work to do at the weekend*)
- **Mae'n well gyda fi goffi na + te > Mae'n well gyda fi goffi na the** (*I prefer coffee to tea,* literally: *it's better with me coffee than tea*)

➤ After the <u>prepositions</u> **tua** (*about/approximately*) and **gyda** (*with*)

- **tua + pum punt ar hugain > tua phum punt ar hugain** (*about twenty-five pounds*)
- **gyda + cyfeillion > gyda chyfeillion** (*with friends*)

➵ Negative <u>short-form</u> verbs beginning with **p, t, c**

- **Prynais i mo'r siaced [prynnais]** *(I didn't buy the jacket)*
- **Thorheulais i ddim ar wyliau [torheulo]** *(I didn't sunbathe on holiday)*
- **Cherddais i ddim i'r gwaith [cerddais]** *(I didn't walk to walk)*

Watcha mas!

There are aspirate mutations after certain <u>particles</u>, e.g.

Ni chân nhw fynd

They won't get to go

Ni triggers aspirate mutation of **p, t, c** and soft mutation of all other consonants in the mutation series. This is known as mixed mutation. The particle **ni** usually gets left out in speech, however, the mutation remains behind.

"Cryptogenic mutations"

Sometimes it looks as though a mutation has snuck in without any apparent cause. We might see a mutation at the start of a sentence or we might see a verb mutated softly in a position we wouldn't expect. Surely these are random and crop up just to confuse learners? Below are some examples of mutations with apparently hidden causes:

1) **Beth wyt ti'n feddwl? [meddwl]**

    What do you think?

2) **Foneddigion a boneddigesau [boneddigion]**

    Ladies and Gentlemen

3) **Fore sul roedd storm yn Sir Benfro [bore]**

    On Sunday morning there was a storm in Pembrokeshire

In 1) we see an example of something your Welsh language tutor will have told you never to do: a mutated verb after **yn**. Don't worry, you haven't been tricked. This sentence has a bit missing.

Beth wyt ti'n feddwl?
What do you think?

Beth	wyt	ti'n	feddwl
What	are	you + yn	think

In spoken Welsh, this sentence appears as in 1), but there's something missing when we compare it to the written or formal version.

Beth wyt ti'n ei feddwl?
What do you think?

Beth	wyt	ti'n	ei	feddwl
What	are	you + yn	his	think

Here the verb *think* (which is a <u>verbal-noun</u>) is being modified by a <u>possessive pronoun</u>. Don't worry about this- it's just something that happens in more formal or written varieties of Welsh. The simple point is that there's a word missing and that in spoken Welsh we often see that the word which originally motivated the mutation has disappeared, leaving a mutated trace.

In 2 we've got a mutation at the very start of the sentence. This is one of the few examples of <u>case</u> in Welsh. The word *ladies* is softly mutated as it's vocative, i.e. it's a word calling for the attention of the listener. Here are some other examples:

- **Fechgyn, dewch 'ma! [bechgyn]**
    - *Boys, come here!*
- **Diolch, bawb [pawb]**
    - *Thanks, everyone*

- **Fadam, allech chi ddiffodd eich sigár? [madam]**
  - *Madam, would you extinguish your cigar?*

In 3 we have a similar situation: a mutation at the start of a sentence without any apparent motivating cause. Here are two more examples of a soft mutation in a similar context:

- **Brynhawn Sul dw i'n mynd mas gyda fy ffrindiau [prynhawn]**
  - *On Sunday afternoon I'm going out with my friends*
- **Mae'r ŵyl yn dechrau ddydd Sul [dydd Sul]**
  - *The festival starts on Sunday*

In these sentences the soft mutation occurs in order to signal the idea of *on* a particular day or during a particular time, e.g. *on Sunday* (i.e. the upcoming one) and not *on Sundays* (i.e. habitually).

There are a few other examples of where a mutation creeps in unexpectedly or isn't motivated by a word that's immediately preceding the mutated one. This can confuse learners who have been given lists of words that cause mutations. Don't panic. If you see a word you can't find in the dictionary, it's probably because it's mutated. You'll need to do some detective work in order to un-mutate the word. Using the rules discussed in this chapter you'll be able to trace the sound back.

Let's look an example. Let's say you come across the following sentence:

Thalaist ti ddim am y bwyd

Let's say you recognise the word for *food* and you've got a feeling that the sentence is negative because you've clocked the mutated form of the word **dim**. You know it's about the second person because you recognise the word **ti**. But that's as far as you've got. You look up **thalaist** in the dictionary and it's not there. If we think about the first sound **th** we can then think about sounds that are similar to it. How can we describe **th**?

- ☐ It's a voiceless/quiet sound (i.e. no voice box buzz)
- ☐ You need your tongue on or near the back of your teeth to make this sound
- ☐ It's a scratchy (i.e. fricative) sound

We could of course just reach for a mutations table, but let's play the linguistic detective. Let's ignore the fricative aspect of this sound for now and think about the other two properties we outlined above. We're looking for a quiet sound pronounced near the teeth. We can't pick any of the following sounds because they're all too divergent from these properties:

	B	**C**	**F**	**Ff**	**P**
Voiceless sound	NO	YES	NO	YES	YES
Pronounced on or near the back of the teeth.	YES	NO	NO	NO	NO

The only sound we can select would be **t** because it's voiceless and pronounced in the same part of the mouth. So the original word is **talaist**. Let's try putting this into our dictionary. We now know it means *you paid*. If you're using a paper dictionary, you could look up the stem **tal-** to find out that the verb is something to do with payment.

Thalaist ti ddim am y bwyd
You didn't pay for the food

The mutations: Be' sy'n bod?

Soft mutations

Below is a series of sentences with the mutation missing. All the words following the bold word should have been softly mutated. Put in the correct soft mutation.

Example: O'n i'n dawnsio'**n** gwyllt *(I was dancing wildly)*
Answer: O'n i'n dawnsio'**n** wyllt

1. Roedd **cath** mawr ar y bwrdd *(There was a big cat on the table)*
2. Aeth e **i** Caerfyrddin *(He went to Carmarthen)*
3. Mae **hen** dyn yn byw drws nesaf *(An old man lives next door)*
4. Roedd **dau** ci gyda nhw *(They had two dogs)*
5. Siwan yw enw **ei** mam e *(His mum's name is Siwan)*
6. Gwelodd **hi** bachgen ar y to *(She saw a boy on the roof)*

Nasal mutations

The following sentences all have incorrect nasal mutations. The original word is given at the end of each sentence. Correct the nasal mutation in each sentence- remember you might also have to change the form of **yn.**

Example: Mae'r cyhoedd yn fy maru! [caru] *(The public love me!)*
Answer: Mae'r cyhoedd yn fy **ngharu**!

1. Dw i'n byw yn Ngaerdydd [Caerdydd] *(I live in Cardiff)*
2. Jon yw enw fy martner [partner] *(Jon is my partner's name)*
3. Caeth hi swydd yn Mhorth [Borth] *(She got a job in Borth)*
4. Mae fy nghesg wrth ymyl y ffenestr [desg] *(My desk is by the window)*
5. Mae ei theulu'n byw yn Mhrefdraeth [Trefdraeth]

   (Her family live in Newport)

6. Mae'r gath yn gorwedd ar fy nghwely [gwely]

   (*The cat's lying on my bed*)

Aspirate mutations

The last set of sentences all have a word that has been mutated softly when it should have been mutated aspirately. Find the incorrectly mutated word, unmutate it and then put in the required aspirate mutation.

Example: Dyn ni'n mynd draw i'w dŷ *(We're going over to her house)*
Answer: **dŷ > tŷ > i'w thŷ**

1. Dyw ei dad ddim yn gwybod am hyn (*Her dad doesn't know about this*)

2. Mae tri gi yn yr ardd (*There are three dogs in the garden*)

3. Siôr ei enw ei bartner (*Siôr is her partner's name*)

4. Coffi a de (*coffee and tea*)

5. Mae ei dractor wedi torri i lawr (*Her tractor's broken down*)

6. Chwe bunt! (*Six pounds!*)

Excuse #2: Saying 'yes' and 'no'

"Bloody hell! Not this again!?"
Intermediate level learner

Yn y bôn

- It's a call-and-response system
- Your answer depends on:
    - Whether the question is emphatic or not
    - The <u>person</u> you're referring to
    - Whether or not the question starts with a verb
        - Whether the verb is a <u>main verb</u> or a form of the verb *to be*

In Welsh, there isn't a single pair of words that corresponds to *yes* and *no*. Your answer depends on who you're referring to, which <u>tense</u> the question is in, the start of the question you're asked and how emphatic you want to be. From an English language perspective, this just sounds insane. Surely *yes* and *no* are universal concepts? When the Martians descend and we examine their language we'll surely discover they can confirm or deny things. We need to be careful here- some grammar books and language teachers like to thrill their learners by saying "there's no word for *yes* or *no* in Welsh!" This is linguistic sensationalism. Of course you can say *yes* and *no* in Welsh. What we're saying is that Welsh has multiple forms of these two words. Not having a single pair of words meaning *yes* and *no* isn't all that rare. Chinese and Japanese also have multiple version of *yes* and *no*. Celtic languages like Welsh, Irish and Scots Gaelic have a call-and-response, or echo, question and answer system.

How you say *yes* or *no* in Welsh depends on the type of question you're asked. Usually it's a case of matching the type of response to the type of question. This means that when we say *yes* or *no* in Welsh, we're really saying something more than just these two words- we're giving extra information and referring back to the event or thing we were asked about. Initially it seems like a minefield and something confabulated to vex learners.

However, sometimes this kind of questioning system removes ambiguity in questions and answers. Let's have a look at an example. Answering a negative question like the one on the following page can be confusing in English because it's never really clear what is being denied.

You don't like learning Welsh? > No

Does this mean that the person replying doesn't like learning Welsh or that that they disagree with the assumption in the question that they don't like learning Welsh?! It's a bit muddled. Whereas in Welsh, it's pretty unambiguous.

Dwyt ti ddim yn hoffi dysgu Cymraeg? > Nac ydw
You don't like learning Welsh? > No (I don't [like learning Welsh])

Present tense questions with *to be*

Yn Saesneg

How to answer the following sorts of questions:
- ***Do you*** live here?
- ***Are you*** happy?
- ***Does she*** like her job?
- ***Do they have*** a turtle?
- ***Is there*** enough bread?
- ***Have you*** seen them?[14]

The first thing you'll do in a beginners' level Welsh class is ask a few question to your fellow learners: *Do you live in London? Do you have any children?* Questions in English often start with the word *do*. However, it's important to appreciate right from the beginning that the grammatical construction of questions in Welsh and English is radically different.

- If you're asked a question using **dych** or **wyt**, you're being asked *do you...?* or *are you...?*
- *Do* and *are* can be translated as the verb *to be*: **dych (chi)** or **wyt (ti)** (there isn't a word corresponding to *do* in Welsh)
- In the first person, you're replying with a form of *yes* which literally means *I am* and a form of *no* which literally means *I am not*.

---

[14] Don't worry! This question is in the past tense, but we'll see later on in this section that it's actually in the present tense in Welsh. Hang on in there!

Questions starting with	Answers
Ydw i? *Am/do I..?*	**Wyt - Nac wyt** *Yes (you are/do) - No (you aren't/don't)* [informal] **Ydych - Nac ydych** *Yes (you are/do) - No (you aren't/don't)* [formal]
Ydyn ni? *Are/do we?*	**Ydyn - Nac ydyn** *Yes (we are/do) - No (we aren't/don't)* **Ydych - Nac ydych** *Yes (you are/do) - No (you aren't/don't)* [plural]
Wyt ti? *Are/do you..?* [informal/singular]	**Ydw - Nac ydw** *Yes (I am/do) - No (I'm not / I don't)*
Dych chi? *Are/do you..?* [formal/plural]	**Ydw - Nac ydw** *Yes (I am/do) - No (I'm not / I don't)* **Ydyn - Nac ydyn** *Yes (we are/do) - No (we aren't/don't)*
Ydy e/hi? *Is/does he/she/it..?*	**Ydy - Nac ydy** *Yes (he/she/it is/does) - No (he/she/it isn't/doesn't)*
Ydyn nhw? *Are/do they..?*	**Ydyn - Nac ydyn** *Yes (they are/do) - No (they aren't/don't)*
Oes? *Is/are there..?*	**Oes - Nac oes** *Yes (there is/are) - No (there isn't/aren't)*

Er enghraifft

Dych chi'n iawn? > ydw
Are you alright? > yes (I am)

Dych chi'n byw yn Llundain? > nac ydw
Do you live in London? > no (I don't)

Ydy e'n hoffi gweithio yng Nghaerdydd? > Nac ydy
Does he like working in Cardiff? > no (he doesn't)

Ydy Mair yn hapus? > ydy
Is Mair happy? > yes (she is)

Watcha mas!

Sometimes you have to answer in the present tense, even if the question is about the past. This is when we have the perfect tense in English.

Wyt ti wedi gweld y ffilm newydd? > ydw
Have you seen the new film > yes [literally: *I am*]

Wyt	ti	wedi	gweld	y	ffilm	newydd
Are	you	PARTICLE	to see	the	film	new

The verb **gweld** (*to see*) is in the infinitive but we know we're talking about the past because we have the past tense particle **wedi**. Because the question word **wyt** is in the present tense, the form of *yes* or *no* we use also has to be in the present tense.

What about **oes**?

- **Oes** means *is there?* or *are there?*
- We use it to ask about possession or ask whether something exists
- You're replying with a form of *yes* that means *there is* or *there are*
- You're replying with a form of *no* that means *there isn't* or *there aren't*

Oes	Nac oes
Yes (there is/are)	No (there isn't/aren't)

Diolch byth!

You don't need to worry about the person of the verb here.

Watcha mas!

When you translate an **oes** question into English, you end up with *do*. However, **oes** isn't *do*- it's a form of the verb *to be* and can be literally translated as *is/are there*.

Oes crwban gyda chi? > oes
Do you have a turtle? > yes (literally: *there is [a turtle with me]*)

Oes	crwban	gyda	chi?
Is there	*a turtle*	*with*	*you?*

Er enghraifft

Oes digon o amser gyda nhw? > nac oes
Do they have enough time? > no

Oes brawd gyda hi o'r enw Siôr? > oes
Does she have a brother called Siôr? > yes

Oes bwyd llysieuol ar y fwydlen? > nac oes
Is there vegetarian food on the menu? > no

Oes teulu gyda nhw yng Nghymru? > oes
Do they have family in Wales? > yes

Past tense with *to be*

Yn Saesneg

How to answer the following sorts of questions:

- ☐ **Were you** happy?
- ☐ **Was she** there?
- ☐ **Was it** raining yesterday?
- ☐ **Did you** know about this?

Questions starting with	Answers
O'n i? *Was I...?*	**O't - Nac o't** *Yes (you were) - No (you weren't)* [informal] **O'ch - Nac o'ch** *Yes (you were) - No (you weren't)* [formal]
O'n ni? *Were we...?*	**O'n - Nac o'n** *Yes (we were) - No (we weren't)* **O'ch - Nac o'ch** *Yes (you were) - No (you weren't)* [plural]
O't ti? *Were you?* [informal/singular]	**O'n - Nac o'n** *Yes (I was) - No (I wasn't)*
O'ch chi? *Were you...?* [formal/plural]	**O'n - Nac o'n** *Yes (I was) - No (I wasn't)* **O'n - Nac o'n** *Yes (we were) - No (we weren't)*
O'dd e/hi? *Was he/she/it...?*	**O'dd - Nac o'dd** *Yes (he/she/it was) - No (he/she/it wasn't)*
O'n nhw? *Were they..?*	**O'n - Nac o'n** *Yes (they were) - No (they weren't)*

Er enghraifft

O't ti'n gwybod am hyn? > o'n
Did you know about this? > yes (I did)

O'n nhw'n mynd i'r parc? > o'n
Were they going to the park? > yes (they were)

O'dd e'n dost? > o'dd
Was he ill? > yes (he was)

O'ch chi'n hapus gyda'r bwyd? > o'n
Were you happy with the food? > yes (we were)

Watcha mas!

There's quite a bit of variation in formality and dialect when it comes to this pair of *yes/no* words. For example, you might hear **nagôt** for **nac o't**, or **na wedd** for **nac o'dd**. No learner, or indeed fluent Welsh speaker, can be expected to know all this regional variation. However, it might be a good idea to familiarize yourself with the formal/written variants. You can see that the spoken/colloquial variants are just shortened versions of the question words and answers in the table below.

Questions starting with	Answers
Oeddwn i? *Was I...?*	**Oeddet - Nac oeddet** *Yes (you were) - No (you weren't)* [*informal*] **Oeddwch - Nac oeddwch** *Yes (you were) - No (you weren't)* [*formal*]

Oedden ni? Were we...?	Oedden - Nac oedden Yes (we were) - No (we weren't) Oeddwch - Nac oeddwch Yes (you were) - No (you weren't) [plural]
Oeddet ti? Were you? [informal/singular]	Oeddwn - Nac oeddwn Yes (I was) - No (I wasn't)
Oeddech chi? Were you...? [formal/plural]	Oeddwn - Nac oeddwn Yes (I was) - No (I wasn't) Oedden - Nac oedden Yes (we were) - No (we weren't)
Oedd e/hi? Was he/she/it...?	Oedd - Nac oedd Yes (he/she/it was) - No (he/she/it wasn't)
Oedden nhw? Were they..?	Oedden - Nac oedden Yes (they were) - No (they weren't)

Past tense without *to be*

Yn y bôn

- If we don't have a form of the verb *to be* at the start of a question, then we need a different pair of words for *yes/no*.
- Here we are talking about questions that start with <u>conjugated</u> verbs and not with the verb *to be*

So far we've been asking questions that start with a form of the verb *to be*:

1. **Wyt ti'n hoffi mynd i Sbaen?** *(Do you like going to Spain?)*
2. **Wyt ti wedi mynd i Sbaen?** *(Have you been to Spain?)*
3. **O't ti'n byw yn Sbaen?** *(Were you living in Spain?)*

Remember that in question 2 we are asking a past <u>tense</u> question but using a present tense form of the verb *to be* (see page 34). But we can also start a question in Welsh by using a <u>main verb</u> at the start of the sentence:

Est ti i'r ysgol ddoe?
Did you go to school yesterday?

Est	ti	i'r	ysgol	ddoe
Went	you	to-the	school	yesterday

Gest ti'r arian wrthi hi?
Did you get the money from her?

Gest	ti'r	arian	wrthi	hi
Got	you-the	money	from [her]	her

Diolch byth!

When a question begins with a <u>main verb</u> in the past <u>tense</u> the forms of *yes* and *no* are the same for all <u>persons</u>, i.e. you don't have to change them depending on who you're referring to.

Do	Naddo
Yes	*No*

Er enghraifft

Est ti i'r ysgol ddoe? > naddo
Did you go to school yesterday?> no (I didn't)

Aeth y rheolwyr am ginio? > do
Did the managers go for lunch?> yes (they did)

Gest ti'r gacen wrthi hi? > naddo
Did you get the cake from her? > no (I didn't)

Gafodd y plant yr arian wrtho fe? > do
Did the children get the money from him? > yes (they did)

Future tense with *to be*

Yn Saesneg

How to answer the following sorts of questions:
- ***Will you** be there?*
- ***Is it going to be** sunny tomorrow?*
- ***Will they** pass the exam?*

Questions starting with	Answers
Fydda i? *Will I (be)...?*	**Byddi - Na fyddi** *Yes (you will) - No (you won't)* [informal] **Byddwch - Na fyddwch** *Yes (you will) - No (you won't)* [formal]
Fyddwn ni? *Will we (be)...?*	**Byddwn - Na fyddwn** *Yes (we will) - No (we won't)* **Byddwch - Na fyddwch** *Yes (you will) - No (you won't)*
Fyddi di? *Will you (be)...?* [informal/singular]	**Bydda - Na fydda** *Yes (I will) - No (I won't)*
Fyddwch chi? *Will you (be)...?* [formal/plural]	**Bydda - Na fydda** *Yes (I will) - No (I won't)* **Byddwn - Na fyddwn** *Yes (we will) - No (we won't)*
Fydd e/hi? *Will he/she/it (be)...?*	**Bydd - Na fydd** *Yes (he/she/it will) - No (he/she/it won't)*
Fyddan nhw? *Will they (be)...?*	**Byddan - Na fyddan** *Yes (they will) - No (they won't)*

Er enghraifft

Fyddi di'n symud tŷ? > bydda
Will you move house? > yes (I will)

Fydd problem? > na fydd
Will there be a problem? > no (there won't be)

Fyddan nhw'n grac? > byddan
Will they be angry? > yes (they will be)

Fyddwn ni'n eu gweld nhw ddydd Sadwrn? > na fyddwn
Will we see them on Saturday? > no (we won't)

1 | Watcha mas!

Remember that you need to reply in the correct <u>person</u>. Look at the following examples:

1. **Fyddwch chi'n mynd i'r parti ddydd Sadwrn? > bydda**
2. **Fyddwch chi'n mynd i'r parti ddydd Sadwrn?> byddwn**

Both sentences have the same question word **fyddwch**, but different answers. Both answers mean *yes*. This is because the formal/singular form of **bydd** is also the <u>plural</u> form. So we use **fyddwch/byddwch** when being respectful to a single person and also when we talk to a group. So we can translate the two questions above as below:

1. *Will you be going to the party on Saturday? > yes (I will)*
2. *Will you be going to the party on Saturday?> yes (we will)*

2 | Watcha mas!

There's a soft mutation to the question word: **byddwch > fyddwch**
Don't worry, head back to Excuse #1 if you're a bit stumped by this.

Conditional tense with *to be*

Yn Saesneg

How to answer the following sort of questions:
- ***Would you*** go there on holiday?
- ***Would he*** know the answer?
- ***Would they*** want to come with us?

Questions starting with	Answers
Fyddwn i? *Would I (be)...?*	**Byddet** - **Na fyddet** *Yes (you would) - No (you wouldn't)* [informal] **Byddech** - **Na fyddech** *Yes (you would) - No (you wouldn't)* [formal]
Fydden ni? *Would we (be)...?*	**Bydden - Na fydden** *Yes (we would) - No (we wouldn't)* **Byddech** - **Na fyddech** *Yes (you would) - No (you wouldn't)*
Fyddet ti? *Would you (be)...?* [informal/singular]	**Byddwn** - **Na fyddwn** *Yes (I would) - No (I wouldn't)*
Fyddech chi? *Would you (be)...?* [formal/plural]	**Byddwn - Na fyddwn** *Yes (I will) - No (I won't)* **Bydden - Na fydden** *Yes (we would) - No (we wouldn't)*
Fyddai fe/hi? *Would he/she/it (be)...?*	**Byddai** - **Na fyddai** *Yes (he/she/it would) - No (he/she/it wouldn't)*
Fydden nhw? *Would they (be)...?*	**Bydden** - **Na fydden** *Yes (they would) - No (they wouldn't)*

Er enghraifft

Fyddet ti'n symud tŷ? > byddwn
Would you move house? > yes(I would)

Fyddai problem? > na fyddai
Would there be a problem?> no (there wouldn't)

Fydden nhw'n grac? > bydden
Would they be angry?> yes (they would)

Fyddwn i'n gallu helpu? > na fyddech
Would I be able to help? > no (you wouldn't)

Cael: *to have/get*

Yn Saesneg

How to answer the following sorts of questions:
- ***May I*** have another cake?
- ***Can we*** use this please?
- ***Will he get*** a job straight away?

Watcha mas!

When **cael** is used in questions asking for permission we can translate it into English as either *can* or *may*. But we can also use **cael** to ask about whether something is going to happen or whether someone is going to get something in the future.

Questions starting with	Answers
Ga(f) i? *May I have/get...?*	**Cei - Na chei** *Yes (you may) - No (you may not)* *[informal]* **Cewch - Na chewch** *Yes(you may) - No (you may not)* *[formal]*
Gawn ni? *May we have/get...?*	**Cewch - Na chewch** *Yes (you may) - No (you may not)* *[plural]*
Gaiff e/hi? *May he/she/it have/get...?*	**Caiff - Na chaiff** *Yes (he/she/it may) - No (he/she/it may)*
Gân nhw? *May they have/get...?*	**Cân - Na chân** *Yes (they may) - No (they may not)*

Er enghraifft

Ga i fwy o win? > cewch
May I have some more wine? > yes (you may)

Gawn ni wybod cyn y parti? > na chewch
Will we get to know before the party? > no (you won't [get to know])

Gân nhw fynd ar y daith hefyd? > cân
Can they go on the trip too? > yes (they can)

Gaiff e gwpan o de? > na chaiff
Can he have a cup of tea? > no (he can't)

Gwneud: *to do/make*

Yn Saesneg

How to answer the following sorts of questions:
- **Will you do** *the homework?*
- **Will you make** *another cake?*

Questions starting with	Answers
Wnei di? *Will you do/make..?* [singular/informal] **Wnewch chi?** *Will you do/make...?* [plural/group]	**Gwnaf - Na wnaf** *Yes (I will do/make) - No (I won't do/make)*

Er enghraifft

Wnei di gacen arall i'r parti? > gwnaf
Will you make another cake for the party? > yes (I will)

Wnewch chi ofyn iddi hi? > na wnaf
Will you ask her? > no (I won't)

Watcha mas!

Often we see **gwneud** being used where we might expect **bydd**, i.e. in questions about the future where we translate the question with *will* at the start. We could also ask the second question above as below:

Fyddwch chi'n gofyn iddi hi?
Will you ask her?

Emphatic questions

Yn y bôn

- These questions are ones that don't start with a verb
- This is another one of the simple exceptions in Welsh's question and answer system where there is a single pair of words for *yes* and *no* within a particular grammatical context.

An emphatic question is one that doesn't start with a question word. Remember that question words are really verbs (usually the verb *to be*). Instead of using a verb at the start of a question we can simply move whatever information we want to emphasise right to the front. You can focus any piece of information by moving it to the start of the question. This makes Welsh have quite a flexible word order, especially as emphatic sentences can be made in any tense.

Diolch byth!

We answer all emphatic questions in the same way irrespective of which person and tense is being used[15].

Ie	Nage
Yes	*No*

Er enghraifft

Tiwtor Cymraeg dych chi? > nage
You're a Welsh tutor? > no

Almaenwr yw ei bartner e? > ie
His partner is German? yes

I'r gwaith aeth hi > nage
She went to work? (literally: to work went she?) > no

---

[15] In North Wales you can hear **ia** and **naci** being used as the emphatic forms instead

Ar y bwrdd o'dd e'n dawnsio? > ie
He was dancing on the table? (literally: on the table was he dancing?) > yes

Nhw o'dd yn creu'r broblem neithiwr? > nage
They were creating the problem last night? > yes

Yn Llundain maen nhw'n dysgu Cymraeg? > ie
They're learning Welsh in London? (literally: in London they are learning Welsh?) > yes

Yes/No: Be' sy'n bod?

Look through the following questions and answers. The answer to each question is the incorrect form of *yes* or *no*. First identify whether the response is positive or negative and then think about what the correct form of *yes* or *no* should be.

1. **Dych chi'n byw yn Llundain? > ie**
2. **Ydyn nhw'n priodi'r flwyddyn nesaf? > ydy**
3. **Oes brawd neu chwaer gyda hi? > nac ydw**
4. **O'dd amser gyda chi ymweld â'r Mont-St-Michel? > oes**
5. **Fyddwn ni'n mynd draw i'w gweld hi ddydd Mawrth? > bydd**
6. **Hi oedd yn y parti? > oedd**
7. **Fydd e eisiau copi o'r llyfr newydd? > na fyddi**
8. **Wnei di baned o de i fi? > nage**
9. **Fyddet ti'n hapus gyda'r syniad? > byddaf**
10. **Fyddai hi eisiau symud i Ddenmarc? > Na fydd**
11. **Ga i edrych? > wyt**
12. **Awdures enwog yw hi? > nac ydy**
13. **Gawn ni fwy o gawl? > na chei**
14. **Wnewch chi ysgrifennu'r cost yma? > ydw**
15. **Yn Llundain maen nhw'n byw? > ydyn**
16. **O'dd Jon yn y parti? > nac oes**

Excuse #3: the verb *to be*

"This verb is a linguistic form of torture"
Upper-intermediate level learner

You need the verb *to be*. It simply cannot be avoided in most languages. It's there in one form or another. However, the verb *to be* can be difficult. In Welsh, you have to juggle with the form of the verb, <u>tense particle</u> and mutations to say the equivalent of *I am* or *I am not*. The verb *to be* can be difficult in any language because it's usually riddled with exceptions. These exceptions manage to stay in the language without being ironed out by linguistic change due to entrenchment. This is the term linguists use to describe words that are used so much that they remain relatively unchanged throughout time despite being exceptions to grammatical rules.

The important thing to remember when you feel your blood pressure begin to rise and sense a slight sweat forming on your brow is that you can deal with exceptions. You speak English and so you know about exceptions in the verb *to be*:

Pronoun	Past tense	Present tense	Future tense
I	was	am	will
We	were	are	will
You	were	are	will
He/she/it	was	is	will
They	were	are	will

It's not as complicated as Welsh, granted, but you can see some exceptions. Compare the system in English to the situation in Swedish and spare a thought for any Swedes learning Welsh.

Pronoun	Past tense	Present tense	Future tense
Jag (*I*)	var	är	ska
Vi (*we*)	var	är	ska
Du/ni (*you*)	var	är	ska
Han/hon/det (*he/she/it*)	var	är	ska
De (*they*)	var	är	ska

"Could be worse" is an important mantra to have when learning another language. Look at the situation in Finnish for the present tense and think to yourself "I can deal with Welsh, it could be so much worse":

English	Finnish
I am	Minä olen
We are	Me olemme
You are	Sinä olet
He/she/it is	Hän on
They are	He ovat

The verb *to be* in Welsh is **bod**. It crops up in this form sometimes, but usually, the form is changed to correspond with the tense (i.e. time) and person (i.e. who we're talking about). We also see some particles being used with the verb *to be*: **yn** and **wedi**. It's important to remember that these particles aren't verbs- instead, they're a bit like the word *do* in English; they don't really have a meaning in and of themselves, but rather stand near verbs to support them. Don't forget to head to the Grammatical Glossary at the back for clear definitions with examples of any underlined grammatical terms.

Below is a table in the first person- i.e. me talking about myself. Included are some useful words to employ when describing how your Welsh class went to friends and family. If you're unsure about the technical grammatical terms for the tense, don't worry about them. Just concentrate on the English examples in italics in the tense column instead.

First person: *I*

Tense	*to be + I*	Particle	Verb example
Present *I am screaming*	**Dw i**	**'n**	**sgrechian**
Imperfect *I was weeping*	**Ro'n i**	**'n**	**wylo**
Future *I will laugh*	**Bydda i**	**'n**	**chwerthin**
Conditional *I would learn*	**Byddwn i**	**'n**	**dysgu**
Perfect *I have shouted*	**Dw i**	**wedi**	**gweiddi**
Pluperfect *I had cried*	**Ro'n i**	**wedi**	**crïo**
Future perfect *I will have read*	**Bydda i**	**wedi**	**darllen**

Watcha mas!

The tables in this Excuse translate present tense sentences as below:

Dw i'n sgrechian

I am screaming

In English, we use -*ing* at the end of verbs when we're talking about things happening now. This is one of the main uses of what's known as the continuous tense in English and it's used an awful lot. However, there isn't anything grammatically continuous about these sentences in Welsh. What we're literally saying is:

Dw	i	'n	sgrechian
Am	I	PARTICLE	to scream

The main verb in Welsh isn't an -*ing* verb, it's actually in the infinitive. No -*ing* like ending has been added- it's not continuous. It's the form we'd get if we looked up this verb in the dictionary, i.e. the form with no endings added. Grammar books usually translate present tense sentences into English with -*ing* at the end of main verbs because we don't actually use the simple present tense forms in English very often. If I say **I run** in English, this doesn't actually mean that I'm running now- instead, I talking about something I habitually do, e.g. **I run at the weekend.** Look at the following pairs of sentences and think about the differences between their uses.

- **I'm running**
    - **I run**
- **I'm working**
    - **I work**

First person plural: *we*

Tense	*to be* + *we*	Particle	Verb example
Present *We are screaming*	**Dyn ni**	'n	sgrechian
Imperfect *We were weeping*	**Ro'n ni**	'n	wylo
Future *We will laugh*	**Byddwn ni**	'n	chwerthin
Conditional *We would learn*	**Bydden ni**	'n	dysgu
Perfect *We have shouted*	**Dyn ni**	wedi	gweiddi
Pluperfect *We had cried*	**Ro'n ni**	wedi	crïo
Future perfect *We will have read*	**Byddwn ni**	wedi	darllen

As you can see by now, the only thing that's changing is the form of the verb *to be* and the pronoun. The particle and the main verb stay exactly the same. When using the verb *to be* with a main verb, it's the verb *to be* that's conjugated and not the other verb in the sentence.

Er enghraifft

Dyn ni'n mynd i'r dref
We're going to town

O'n ni wedi cael digon
We'd had enough

Ro'n ni'n byw drws nesaf iddyn nhw

We lived next door to them

Bydden ni'n hapus i'ch helpu

We'd be happy to help you

Second person: *you*

Tense	formal/plural *to be + you*	informal/singular *to be + you*	Particle
Present *You are*	**Dych chi**	**Rwyt ti**	'n
Imperfect *You were*	**Ro'ch chi**	**Ro't ti**	'n
Future *You will*	**Byddwch chi**	**Byddi di**	'n
Conditional *You would*	**Byddech chi**	**Byddet ti**	'n
Perfect *You have*	**Dych chi**	**Rwyt ti**	wedi
Pluperfect *You had*	**Ro'ch chi**	**Rwyt ti**	wedi
Future perfect *You will have*	**Byddwch chi**	**Byddi di**	wedi

Er enghraifft

Dych chi'n edrych yn wych!
You look great!

Ro'ch chi'n arfer cwrdd â nhw'n aml
You used to meet them often

Byddwch chi wedi gweld y sioe cyn i fi ei gweld
You'll have seen the show before I see it

Byddech chi'n hapus iawn yno
You'd be very happy there

Third person: *he/she, they*

Tense	Singular to be + he/she/it	Plural to be + they	Particle
Present *He/she/it*	**Mae e/hi**	**Maen nhw**	'n
Imperfect *He/she/it was*	**Roedd e/hi**	**Ro'n nhw**	'n
Future *He/she/it will*	**Bydd e/hi**	**Byddan nhw**	'n
Conditional *He/she/it would*	**Byddai e/hi**	**Bydden nhw**	'n
Perfect *He/she/it has*	**Mae e/hi**	**Maen nhw**	wedi
Pluperfect *He/she/it had*	**Roedd e/hi**	**Ro'n nhw**	wedi
Future perfect *He/she/it will have*	**Bydd e/hi**	**Byddan nhw**	wedi

Er enghraifft

Roedd e'n mynd draw i'w gweld hi
He was going over to see her

Maen nhw wedi cael digon
They've had enough

Bydd gormod o bobl yn y parti
There'll be too many people at the party

Byddai'r staff yn hapus
The staff will be happy

Watcha mas!

It's very common for learners to make the following kind of error with the third person plural (i.e. *they*):

*****Roedden y plant yn chwarae** *(The children were playing)*

Here, the plural form of the verb *to be* has been used with a plural noun. Logically this might make sense. But we're dealing with a real language here and so logic doesn't always play much of a role. If you've studied some German you'll know that number is encoded in verbs, i.e. the verb form tells us whether the subject is one person or more than one person.

English	German	Welsh
The children played	Die Kinder spielten	Chwareodd y plant
They played	Sie spielten	Chwaraeon nhw
He played	Er spielte	Chwaerodd e

In Welsh, verbs aren't encoded for number consistently in a way similar to German. German has the plural ending -ten if the subject is plural- it doesn't matter whether the pronoun they is used or whether a plural noun (e.g. children) is used instead- the ending's the same. In Welsh, however we use **-odd** for third person subjects and it doesn't matter whether these are plural or singular. However, when we use they word **nhw** (*they*), then we use a different ending with the verb. So in Welsh, what's important is not number, but person. English is a different situation altogether- English verbs are so boring. You can just whack *played* with any pronoun as long as the sentence is in the past, so the idea of number doesn't really exist in main verbs used to talk about the past in English.

The present tense form **mae** and the past tense form **roedd** can be used when the subject is a single person or many people. **Mae** means *is* and *are* and **roedd** means *was* and *were*

- **Roedd plant yn sefyll ar y ddesg** (*children were standing on the desk*)
- **Roedd bachgen yn sefyll ar y ddesg** (*a boy was standing on the desk*)

The verb ending **-en** is only used when the pronoun **nhw** (*they*) is used:

- ***Roedden plant yn sefyll ar y ddesg**
- **Roedden nhw'n sefyll ar y ddesg**

What about **yw**?

Look at the two sentences below. The verb *to be* is different in Welsh but there's no difference when these sentences are translated into English.

1. **Athro yw e**

    He's a teacher
2. **Mae e'n canu**

    He's singing

Sentence 2 contains a <u>main verb</u> underway at the time of speaking, i.e. *he's singing now*. The verb appears with the present tense <u>particle</u> **yn**. But in the first sentence we don't have the <u>affirmative</u> third <u>person</u> **mae** that we've just seen in the tables above. Why? One reason is that sentence 1 is emphatic; it has new information at the start instead of a verb. Remember that **yn** can only appear before <u>predicates</u> that are actions underway or descriptions of physical/mental properties (see the section on <u>particles</u> in the Grammatical Glossary). Where we don't have an action underway and we are also usually being empathic, we use special emphatic forms of the verb *to be*, **yw**, in the third <u>person</u>. It might help to think of it like this: when using the third <u>person</u>, **yw** goes with <u>nouns</u>, whilst **mae** and its friend **yn** go with verbs and descriptions.

1 | Watcha mas!

Whilst third <u>person</u> **yw** is very different to **mae**, there isn't always a separate emphatic form of the verb *to be* used when there is no main verb in the sentence. Sometimes it's just the order that's changed.

Gweinidog dych chi (*You're a minister*)
Dych chi'n byw ar gwch (*You live on a boat*)

Sometimes the forms are practically the same. Note that in the second sentence on the next page, some people in some parts of Wales would just use the same form of the verb *to be* as the first sentence (**Cymro dw i**). Whilst the words might be the same, it's important to recognize that what's the same few words in English, *I am*, is actually conveying two different concepts: a statement of fact versus a description of an action underway.

Dw i'n gweithio nawr
I'm working now

Cymro ydw i
I'm a Welshman

2 | Watcha mas!

We said above that **yw** is a third <u>person</u> form, i.e. for talking about other people outside of the conversation (*he, she,* etc.). This isn't strictly true. The following is a perfectly grammatical sentence:

Fi yw'r gorau!
I'm the best! (It is I who is the best!)

Sydd yn/sy'n

Sydd, or the shortened form **sy**, is a form of the verb *to be* which has two different uses. Firstly, it crops up in sentences where the subject is emphasised to some degree. In these kinds of sentences there isn't a verb in the first position of the sentence:

Jon sy'n ennill!
Jon wins! / Jon's winning / it's Jon who's winning

The second use of **sydd** is as a relative pronoun- this means a word that joins two bits of a sentence together. When it's used like this we can translate it as *which/who/that is/are.*

Dyma'r dyn sydd yn cwyno
Here's the man who's complaining

Certain question words also require the relative pronoun **sydd** to be placed after them, e.g. **pwy** (*who*). But watch out! **Pwy** can be followed by either **yw** or **sydd** in the present <u>tense</u> depending on whether there's an action underway or a description following:

Pwy yw'r enillydd?
Who's the winner?

Pwy sy'n ennill?
Who's winning?

`Er enghraifft`

Fe sy'n gyrru
He's driving ("It's he who is driving")

Y plant sy'n ffraeo yw'r broblem
It's the kids who are arguing who are the problem

Pwy sy'n gwybod yr ateb?
Who knows the answer?

Dych chi'n gweld y cwch sydd ar y llyn?
Do you see the boat that's on the lake?

Beth sy'n bod arnoch chi?
What's wrong with you?

Negatives

`Yn y bôn`

- ☐ You need to mark negative sentences as negative twice
- ☐ The verb *to be* will change (either completely or it'll mutate)

Negating a form of the verb *to be* is easy as long as you remember that you need to mark the sentence as negative twice, i.e. you need two negative parts in the sentence. First, you need to select a negative form of the verb *to be*: sometimes this means selecting a different form of the verb *to be* altogether and sometimes you just need to mutate the form of the verb *to be* you'd use in an affirmative sentence. Secondly, you need a mutated form of the negative element **dim.** Here are some example sentences in the first, second and third person with the two negative elements highlighted. Remember: two negatives in Welsh make a negative!

1. **Dw** i **ddim** yn hoffi rygbi (*I don't like rugby*)
2. **Fydda** i **ddim** yn mynd ar wyliau eleni (*I won't go on holiday this year*)
3. **Dwyt** ti **ddim** wedi gwneud dy waith cartref (*You haven't done your homework*)
4. **Fyddech** chi **ddim** yn hapus yn y swydd 'na (*You wouldn't be happy in that job*)
5. **Dyw** e **ddim** yn byw yn Lloegr (*He doesn't live in England*)
6. **Doedd** y **tiwtor** ddim yn hapus (*The tutor wasn't happy*)

In sentences 3, 5 and 6 we have a different form of the verb *to be* for the negative, whereas in sentences 2 and 4 we have a softly mutated form of the <u>affirmative</u> verb *to be*. In all examples, the negative element **dim** is directly next to the <u>subject</u> and is mutated softly.

Watcha mas!

We said above that, contrary to the laws of science, two negatives make a negative in Welsh and that we need two negative elements in a sentence in order to make it negative. But it looks like this hasn't happened in the first sentence below:

1. **Dw** i **ddim** yn hoffi rygbi (*I don't like rugby*)
2. **Dw i'n hoffi rygbi** (*I like rugby*)

Sentence 1 is negative and sentence 2 is <u>affirmative</u>, however, they both start with the same form of the verb *to be*. How does this work? Well, opaquely sentence 1 does, in fact, contain a negative form of the verb *to be*. Look at the table below, it contains the <u>affirmative</u> and negative forms of the verb *to be* in the first <u>person</u>, i.e. *I am* and *I am not*. The forms at the top are the older/literary forms and the forms nearer the bottom are more modern/colloquial forms.

Yr wyf yn	Nid wyf yn
Rwyf yn	Dwyf ddim yn
Rydw i'n	Dydw i ddim yn
Dw i'n	Dw i ddim yn

As the forms of *to be* have been simplified over the decades, we've ended up with <u>affirmative</u> and negative forms of the verb *to be* looking exactly the same. However, once we know how we ended up at this point it might seem slightly less confusing.

First person: *I*

Tense	to be + I	Particle	Verb example
Present *I am not screaming*	**Dw i**	ddim yn	sgrechian
Imperfect *I was not weeping*	**Do'n i**	ddim yn	wylo
Future *I will not laugh*	**Fydda i**	ddim yn	chwerthin
Conditional *I would not learn*	**Fyddwn i**	ddim yn	dysgu
Perfect *I have not shouted*	**Dw i**	ddim wedi	gweiddi
Pluperfect *I had not cried*	**Do'n i**	ddim wedi	crïo
Future perfect *I will not have read*	**Fydda i**	ddim wedi	darllen

Second person: *you*

Tense	formal/plural *to be* + *you* + negative	informal/singular *to be* + *you* + negative	Particle
Present *You are not*	**Dych chi ddim**	**Dwyt ti ddim**	**yn**
Imperfect *You were not*	**Do'ch chi ddim**	**Do't ti ddim**	**yn**
Future *You will not*	**Fyddwch chi ddim**	**Fyddi di ddim**	**yn**
Conditional *You would not*	**Fyddech chi ddim**	**Fyddet ti ddim**	**yn**
Perfect *You have not*	**Dych chi ddim**	**Dwyt ti ddim**	**wedi**
Pluperfect *You had not*	**Do'ch chi ddim**	**Dwyt ti ddim**	**wedi**
Future perfect *You will not have*	**Fyddwch chi ddim**	**Fyddi di ddim**	**wedi**

Third person: *he/she, they*

Tense	Singular *to be + he/she/it*	Plural *to be + they*	Particle
Present *He/she/it is not*	**Dyw e/hi ddim**	**Dyn nhw ddim**	yn
Imperfect *He/she/it was not*	**Doedd e/hi ddim**	**Do'n nhw ddim**	yn
Future *He/she/it will not*	**Fydd e/hi ddim**	**Fyddan nhw ddim**	yn
Conditional *He/she/it would not*	**Fyddai e/hi ddim**	**Fydden nhw ddim**	yn
Perfect *He/she/it has not*	**Dyw e/hi ddim**	**Dyn nhw ddim**	wedi
Pluperfect *He/she/it had not*	**Doedd e/hi ddim**	**Do'n nhw ddim**	wedi
Future perfect *He/she/it will not have*	**Fydd e/hi ddim**	**Fyddan nhw ddim**	wedi

Sa, so, so, so, so, so

You may have heard or perhaps seen sentences like the following:

- **Sa i'n gwybod!** (*I don't know!*)
- **So fe'n mynd i basio'r arholiad** (*He's not going to pass the exam*)
- **So nhw'n mynd i'r parti** (*They're not going to the party*)

Welsh is a living language and as such its grammar, just like English's, is in a constant state of flux; things are changing. We're currently seeing a radical simplification of negative sentence patterns in Welsh in which they only contain 1 negative element.

I'm not	**Sa i'n**
We're not	**So ni'n**
You're not [formal/plural]	**So chi'n**
You're not [informal/singular]	**So ti'n**
He/she/it isn't	**So fe/hi'n**
They aren't	**So nhw'n**

Speakers of Welsh (particularly in the south) are increasingly saying and writing the forms above instead of those we've seen in previous sections of this Excuse. The new, emerging system definitely looks simpler; however, some purists consider it an aberration that needs firmly underlining in red. But remember, you're learning Welsh which makes you a linguistic stakeholder so it's up to you which you use! **Sa i'n mynd i jydjo ti!**

What about *bu*?

Is it the present perfect continuous? Shall we translate it as *do?* Should it be labelled the 'preterite form of *to be*'? How about the 'episodic past'? Grammar does matter because, as David Crystal says, "it's there"[16]. Knowing some grammatical terms does mean you can learn with insight as opposed to just learning by rote. It's like knowing what the Latin terms mean when you're studying an anatomy exam. Having said that, I think that sentences like **bues i'n hwylio ar Fôr y Canoldir** are best understood not by whacking a grammatical label onto them, but by understanding the contexts of their uses and the additional meanings they convey. Whatever you call it, **bu** is a form of the verb *to be* and it's one of the forms of the verb we can use to talk about things in the past. The following sentences are all about walking in the Preseli Mountains. They all happened in the past and they are all in the first person. Sentences 2 and 3 both

---

[16] Crystal, D. 2004. *Rediscover Grammar.* Longman Pearson.

have a past tense form of the verb *to be* in them, but sentence 3 has an additional layer of meaning.

1. **Cerddais i ym Mynyddoedd y Preseli**

   Someone asks you what you did yesterday afternoon and you answer with this sentence. You went walking yesterday afternoon for a few hours and then you came back.

2. **O'n i'n cerdded ym Mynyddoedd y Preseli**

   You've been out walking all day, from dawn 'til dusk. You get back and someone asks you **Ble o't ti heddiw?** *(Where were you today?)*, you answer with sentence number 2.

3. **Bues i'n cerdded ym Mynyddoedd y Preseli**

   You've taken a week out of your schedule to go walking in the Preseli Mountains. You have camped in a tent on Carningli and gone all Waldo Williams writing your next Eisteddfod banger. You go back to work and after a week a busybody asks you by the kettle, **ble o't ti'r wythnos ddiwethaf, te?** *(Where were you last week, then?)* and you answer with sentence number 3.

Bu is used in the past tense with the particle **yn** and the verb in the infinitive when talking about something that began and ended in the past and that lasted for a set period. Usually this set period is a few days. This is the kind of verb you'd use when talking about a holiday or to refer to a time several years ago when you did a different job or lived in a different place. It conveys the idea of a set period of time that began and ended in the past in which you continuously did something.

Pronoun	Affirmative	Negative	Interrogative
I	Bues i'n	Fues i ddim yn	Fues i'n
We	Buon ni'n	Fuon ni ddim yn	Fuon ni'n
You [informal/singular]	Buest ti'n	Fuest ti ddim yn	Fuest ti'n
You [formal/plural]	Buoch chi'n	Fuoch chi ddim yn	Fuoch chi'n
He/she/it	Buodd e/hi'n	Fuodd e/hi ddim yn	Fuodd e/hi'n
They	Buon nhw'n	Fuon nhw ddim yn	Fuon nhw'n

Er enghraifft

Buodd hi'n gweithio yn Seland Newydd
+> She was working in New Zealand sometime in the past and was there for a quite a while.

Fuon nhw ddim yn hapus iawn yno
+> They weren't very happy there for a set period which began and ended in the past.

Bues i'n hwylio ar Fôr y Canoldir ym mis Awst
+> I was sailing in the Mediterranean and it lasted for most or all of August- I want you to know I can sail properly and that I've got a yacht.

Buoch chi'n gymwys iawn yn eich gwaith
+> for a period in the past you were very competent in your work, but now you've rather let yourself go professionally.

The verb *to be*: Be' sy'n bod?

Below is a series of <u>affirmative</u> and negative sentences. In each sentence one of three possible errors has occurred:

- The <u>particle</u> **yn** or **wedi** is in the wrong place
- The verb *to be* is in the incorrect <u>person</u>
- The verb *to be* is not in the correct positive or negative form
- A mutation is missing or incorrect
- There's a negative element missing or erroneously added

1. **Dw i'n ddim yn mynd** (*I'm not going*)
2. **Bydd e ddim yn hapus** (*He won't be happy*)
3. **Ro't chi'n arfer byw yn y Ffindir** (*You used to live in Finland*)
4. **Mae hi ddim wedi ennill** (*She hasn't won*)
5. **Fydd y coleg ar gau** (*The college will be closed*)
6. **Dwyt ti'n gwybod** (*You don't know*)
7. **Fydd nhw ddim yn gallu eich helpu** (*They won't be able to help you*)
8. **Dyw e'n gallu chwarae'r delyn** (*He can't play the harp*)
9. **Roedden y plant ar wyliau** (*The children were on holiday*)
10. **Dw i dim yn gweld y pwynt** (*I can't see the point*)

Grammatical Glossary

Here's the glossary. It's arranged alphabetically and contains definitions and examples of all the underlined grammatical terms used throughout the book. In the examples, the grammatical elements under consideration are underlined.

Adjectives

Adjectives describe nouns (i.e. things, places or people).

Y gath ddu

The *black* cat

Syniad ofnadwy

A *terrible* idea

Pobl erchyll

Horrendous people

Mae'n wych

It's *great*

In Welsh, adjectives almost always come after the noun they describe (which is the opposite of English). **Hen** (*old*) is an example of an adjective which always comes before the noun, e.g. **hen ddyn** (*old* man). When adjectives precede the noun they describe they cause a soft mutation. However, there aren't many which precede the noun like this. Here are some others:

- **Ambell** (*some, few*)
- **Cam** (*wrong, unjust*)
- **Cryn** (*a good, quite a, considerable*)
- **Gau** (*false*)
- **Gwir** (*true, genuine*)
- **Prif** (*chief, main*)
- **Unig** (*only, lone*)

If an adjective describes a singular feminine noun (see below) then it mutates softly, e.g. **cath + du > cath ddu** (*black* cat).

Sometimes there are separate feminine forms of adjectives, e.g. **cath wen** (*white cat*) versus **ci gwyn** (*white dog*).

When we're describing something using the verb *to be* we need to use the particle **yn** and softly mutate the adjective, e.g. **mae'n wych** (*it's great*).

Adverb/adverbially

Adverbs describe verbs (i.e. actions). They tell us something about the quality of an action.

Rhedodd y fenyw i lawr y stryd yn gyflym
The woman ran down the street quickly

Meddyliodd y dyn yn hiraethus am ei wlad
The man thought longingly about his country

Gyrrodd y car heibio'n araf
The car drove slowly past

In English, adverbs have a particular ending, *-ly,* which distinguishes them from adjectives. In Welsh, they don't have a separate form from adjectives and still take the particle **yn** as adjectives do. English adverbs can mostly go before or after the verb they describe: *the teacher screamed loudly* versus *the teacher loudly screamed*. In Welsh, adverbs almost always appear in the following order:

Sgrechodd yr athro'n uchel
The teacher screamed loudly/ the teacher loudly screamed

Sgrechodd	yr	athro'n	uchel
verb + third person past ending	definite article	subject + particle	adverb

Affirmative

Affirmative is the opposite of negative. Affirmative refers to verbs which are used to describe something that's actually happening, i.e. is true and not being denied. It's just another word for positive.

Dw i'n dwli ar gaws!
I am mad about cheese!

Bydda i yno!
I'll be there!

Case

Case is the word given to a category of nouns whose form tells us something about that word's role in the sentence. Distinctive forms for grammatical case perished in English hundreds of years ago. However, a few examples remain e.g.

1. *He* said *he* gave the book to *him*
2. *She* saw *them*
3. The school has lost *its* funding
4. No-one knew it was *theirs*

Sentences 1 and 2 have examples of the nominative and objective case. We can't use the same word for the person giving the object and the person receiving it, e.g. **he said he gave the book to he.* Instead the person getting the book has their pronoun in the objective case (*me, him, her, them*).

In sentences 3 and 4 we have examples of the genitive case; *its* and *theirs* give us information about possession.

There are a few more examples, e.g. the increasingly old-fashioned and pompous sounding *by whom* or *to whom it may concern.*

In Welsh, we don't really have to worry about case at all. Sometimes we see a soft mutation for the vocative case (see Excuse #1), i.e. when someone's attention is being called:

Fadam, cywilydd arnoch!
Madam, shame on you!

Direct objects (see below) also mutate softly in Welsh which we could think of as the dative case e.g.

Gwelodd hi long [llong]
She saw a ship

Really though, there isn't case in Welsh. Even less of it than there is in English.

Compound words

These are words made by sticking two words together.

Heddlu (*police*) = **Hedd** (*peace*) + **llu** (*force*)
Llanelli = **Llan** (*parish*) + **Elli** (Saint Elli)
Melyngoch (*orange*) = **melyn** (*yellow*) + **coch** (*red*)
Rheithgor (*jury*) = **rhaith** (*law*) + **côr** (*choir*)

The second part of compound words usually softly mutates. Sometimes the constituents of the compound might have slightly different forms when compared to the dictionary entries of the word, e.g. **rheith~rhaith, côr~cor.**

Conjugation

Conjugated words are ones which have taken a form which give information about (amongst other things) person and tense. They're different from infinitive verbs.

Dw i'n mynd nawr
I'm going now

Gwrandawais i arno
I listened to him

Sometimes a word might be conjugated in English but not in Welsh and vice versa. In the first sentence above, the word *to go* appears in its conjugated form *going*, however this verb isn't conjugated in the equivalent Welsh sentence. Welsh also conjugates prepositions, e.g. the word **ar** (*on*) appears in the conjugated form **arno** (*on him*) in the second sentence above.

Conjunctions

These words are a bit like grammatical glue- they join words, phrases and sentences together.

Bydd rhai yn mynd ar y bws a bydd y lleill yn cerdded
Some will go on the bus and the others will walk

Naill ai mae Jon yn hwyr neu mae e wedi anghofio
Jon's either late or he's forgotten

Definite article

The word that comes before a noun and makes it specific/definite.

Y llyfr
The book

There are 3 forms of the definite article in Welsh:

Y	Before words beginning with a consonant **Y bachgen** *The boy*
Yr	Before words beginning with a vowel **Yr ysgol** *The school*
'r	Added onto words ending in a vowel **Mae'r bws 'ma!** *The bus is here!*

Unlike other European languages like French or German, there aren't separate forms of the definite article for masculine and feminine nouns. The three different forms of the definite article given above can appear with nouns of either grammatical gender. When the definite article appears before a singular feminine noun (see below) it triggers a soft mutation (**y + desg > y ddesg**).

Interrogative

Interrogative describes a sentence that asks a question. Certain words in a sentence might help convey the idea of interrogation:

Pwy dych chi?
Who are you?

Dych chi'n byw yma?
Do you live here?

We can mark short-form verbs as interrogative by mutating them softly.

Fwytaist ti ar y trên?
Did you eat on the train?

Fwytaist	ti	ar	y	trên?
Ate	you	on	the	train?

In English, we can make a statement into a question by using *do* and changing the word order around a bit. This isn't the case in Welsh, where the usual word order is VERB SUBJECT OBJECT in questions and in statements. In the examples below, it would only be the context or the questioner's intonation that would tell you whether a question was being asked.

Est ti i'r dref
You went to town

Est ti i'r dref?
Did you go to town?

However, in the sentences below the verb starts with a consonant that can be mutated. Here the distinction between statements and questions is indicated by the presence of a soft mutation.

Torraist ti'r ffenestr 'ma
You broke this window

Dorraist ti'r ffenestr 'ma
Did you break this window?

Noun

A noun is a place, a person or a thing.

Athrawes (*female teacher*)
Desg (*desk*)
Rhufain (*Rome*)
Tŷ (*house*)

Nouns in Welsh are either masculine or feminine (see the section on singular feminine nouns below). Whether a word is feminine or masculine determines the mutations it takes and causes.

Number (plural)

Grammatical number is the property of the word which tells us how many there are of something. English only shows plural number on nouns (*dog, dog<u>s</u>*) and the verb *to be* (he <u>is</u>, they <u>are</u>), however, Welsh marks plural number on other parts of the sentence too.

Mae <u>plant</u> ar y to!
There <u>are</u> <u>children</u> on the roof!

Mae plentyn ar y to!
There is a child on the roof!

Mae <u>llawer</u> o <u>fynyddoedd</u> <u>mawrion</u> yn y wlad
There <u>are</u> <u>many</u> large <u>mountains</u> in the country

Languages mark things as plural and singular in different ways and sometimes words don't specify number at all. **Mae** can be translated as either *are* or *is*. However, we do see separate forms of verbs used with plurals when the pronoun **nhw** (*they*) is used, e.g. **Edrychon nhw ar y llun** (*They looked at the picture*) compared with **Roedd y myfyrwyr yn edrych ar y llun** (*The students were looking at the picture*).

Object

This is the name for the part of the sentence that's affected by the verb. In English, these come after the verb. This book has mentioned two types of object: direct and indirect.

Direct Object

Torrodd y bachgen y ffenestr
The boy broke the window

Torrodd	y bachgen	y ffenestr
main verb	subject	direct object

In Welsh, the direct object is softly mutated if it's immediately next to the subject.

Brathodd y ci fachgen [bachgen]
The dog bit a boy

Indirect Object

Indirect objects are usually animate beings to which something happens or to whom something is given, i.e. they're the recipients of something.

Rhoddodd hi'r gacen i'r ci
She gave the dog the cake

Rhoddodd	hi	'r gacen	i	'r ci
main verb	subject	direct object	preposition	indirect object

Particle

Welsh has two kinds of tense particles that appear with the verb *to be*.

yn / 'n	present tense particle
wedi	past tense particle

Mae Gwen yn rhedeg
Gwen's running

Mae hi wedi mynd
She's gone

The present tense particle **yn** appears before actions underway (e.g. sentence 1 below) or descriptions of physical/mental attributes (e.g. sentence 2 below).

1. **Mae Jon yn gyrru'r car** *(Jon is driving the car)*

2. **Mae Jon yn hyll** *(Jon is ugly)*

When **yn** appears after a word ending in a vowel it's shortened to '**n**

Mae e'n rhedeg
He's running

There are some other particles that appear occasionally, but which are increasingly confined to written and formal varieties of Welsh or frozen in certain phrases:

Ni	negative particle	**Ni chaniateir ysmygu** *Smoking is not permitted*
A	question particle	**A oes heddwch?** *Is there peace?*
Bu	past tense particle	**Bu farw Hedd Wyn yn 1917** *Hedd Wyn died in 1917*
Fe	pre-verbal particle	**Fe fydd problemau** *There will be problems*

1 | Watcha mas!

Yn can mean two things: the tense particle discussed here or it can mean *in*. The sentence below has both types of **yn** in it:

Mae'r teulu'n byw yng Nghatalwnia
The family lives in Catalonia

When you use **yn** as a preposition it can't be shortened to '**n** and added to the subject:

*Dw i'n Sbaen
*I'm Spain

Dw i yn Sbaen
I'm in Spain

2 | Watcha mas!

The tense particles **yn** and **wedi** can't appear together:

*Dw i'n wedi blino
* I'm was tired
Dw i wedi blino (*I'm tired*, literally: *I have tired*)

Person

This is the property of the verb which tells us something about who is being spoken about.

First person	Me talking about me	**Dw i'n hoffi coffi** *I like coffee*
Second Person	Me talking to you about you	**Rwyt ti'n hoffi coffi** *You like coffee*
Third person	Me talking to you about someone else	**Mae hi'n hoffi coffi** *She likes coffee*

Predicatively/predicate

The predicate is the part of the sentence that tells us something about the subject.

Mae e'n llwyddiannus iawn
He's very successful

Roedd y dorf yn canu
The crowd were singing

In Welsh, adjectives used predicatively mutate softly after the particle **yn**

Ydy'r rheolwr yn grac? [crac]
Is the manager angry?

Prepositions

Prepositions tell us something about the relationship between two things or parts of a sentence.

Aeth hi i Gaerdydd
She went to Cardiff

Bwyton ni mewn bwyty hyfryd
We ate in a lovely restaurant

Mae gweddill y tîm ar gopa'r mynydd yn barod!
The rest of the team are already at the summit!

Ygrifennwyd y llyfr gan awdur enwog
The book was written by a famous author

Prepositions in Welsh conjugate to correspond with the required person. This means that pronouns can be dropped from sentences.

Dyma'r llun ohono/ohoni
This is the picture of him/her

ohona i	from/of me
ohonon ni	from/of us
ohonot[17] ti	from/of you [informal/singular]
ohonoch chi	from/of you [formal/plural]
ohoni hi	from/of her
ohono fe	from/of him
ohonyn nhw	from/of them

---

[17] **Ohonat ti** is another possibility here

Pronouns

Pronouns are small words that stand in for names in a sentence.

Fe sy'n mynd i'w casglu nhw cyn y parti
He's the one collecting them before the party

Dw i heb gael cyfle i siarad â hi eto
I haven't had chance to talk to her yet

English	Welsh	Emphatic pronouns
I/me	fi	A finnau
We/us	ni	A ninnau
You	Ti [informal/singular] Chi [formal/plural]	A thithau A chithau
He/him	Fe[18]	Ac yntau
She/her	Hi	A hithau
They/them	Nhw	A hwythau

Possessive pronouns

Possessive pronouns tell us about ownership

English	Welsh	Mutation/sound addition
My	Fy	Nasal mutation **fy mrawd** (*my brother*)
Our	Ein	+ h [words beginning with a vowel] **ein hysgol** (*our school*)
Your [informal/singular]	Dy	Soft mutation **dy fam** (*your mum*)
Your [formal/plural]	Eich	No mutation/change

---

[18] **Fe** often appears as **e**. In the North, **fo** or **o** is used instead.

His	**Ei**	Soft mutation **ei dad** (*his dad*)
Her	**Ei**	aspirate mutation **ei thad** (*her dad*)
Its	**Ei**	Masculine nouns: soft mutation Feminine nouns: aspirate mutation
Their	**Eu**	+h [words beginning with a vowel] **eu hymdrechion** (*their efforts*)

Singular feminine nouns

Nouns in Welsh, like in the majority of European languages, are divided into different categories. Welsh nouns are either masculine or feminine. This isn't to do with whether the nouns are masculine or feminine things; it's just what the categories are called. Some languages call their noun categories 'common' and 'neuter' (like Dutch and Swedish), Welsh and French call them masculine and feminine.

Singular feminine nouns have two grammatical properties encoded in them: they are singular (referring to one thing only) and they are part of the feminine category of nouns. These words are softly mutated when preceded by the definite article. They also cause a soft mutation to adjectives.

Roedd y gath ddu yn eistedd wrth ymyl y tân [cath + du]
The black cat was sitting by the fireside

Ysgol fawr iawn yw hi
It's a very large school

Subject

The subject is usually the animate being carrying out an action.

Mae Gwen yn dawnsio ar y ford
Gwen is dancing on the table

Fydden nhw'n ddim yn gallu fforddio'r tŷ 'na
They wouldn't be able to afford that house

Roedd aelodau'r tîm yn grac iawn
The members of the team were very angry

Tense

Tense is the word for the property of a verb which tells us something about when an action happened or is happening.

Present tense
This refers to things happening now, in the present moment.

Wyt ti'n wallgo?
Are you mad?

Mae'r ci'n cysgu
The dog is sleeping

Jon yw enw ei phartner
Jon is her partner's name

Perfect tense

This is the tense which describes an action started in the past and continuing up to the present. It can also be used to talk about events in the past without being specific about the time in which they occurred. Some grammar books don't refer to this as a tense and prefer to call it the 'perfective aspect'. Whatever you call it, a spade is still a shovel as far as I'm concerned. In English, the perfect tense involves the verb *have* in some form.

Dw i wedi byw yma ers achau
I've lived here for ages

Dych chi wedi gweld y ffilm newydd?
Have you seen the new film?

Mae e wedi bod i America
He's been to America

Main verbs in most varieties of "standard" English have a separate form for the perfect tense (e.g. *I have seen* versus **I have saw*).

Verbs

Verbs are actions or "doing words". There a lots of different types of verb, e.g. the verb *to be* (see Excuse #3), main verbs or verbal-nouns. The word verb is really a category term for this part of speech.

Infinitive

The infinitive is the most basic form of the verb, i.e. it's not conjugated and doesn't have any endings added. In English, this corresponds to verbs with *to* in front of them, e.g. *to sing*. In Welsh, the infinitive is used when it isn't in English:

Dw i'n <u>mynd</u> i'r siop nawr
I'm going to the shop now

The following sentence contains a very common error that learners make. Here **i** has been added to make the English-style infinitive *to sing*

*Gofynna iddo fe i ganu!
Ask him to sing!

The sentence above actually has a verbal-noun and not an infinitive. See the verbal- nouns section below for an explanation.

Main verb

This is a type of verb that gives information about an action. Some verbs tell us information the likelihood that an action will happen or the speaker's opinion about the action being described (e.g. *should, would, can*); these kinds of verbs support other verbs. But main verbs are any verbs that just tell us about something that's physically (or mentally happening).

Ydy e'n <u>dawnsio</u>?
Is he <u>dancing</u>?

Ga i <u>edrych</u>?
Can I <u>see</u>?

Mae'r gath yn <u>eistedd</u> ar y gadair
The cat's <u>sitting</u> on the chair

Dw i ddim yn meddwl amdano
I'm not thinking about it

Bydd Gwen yn rhedeg marathon eleni
Gwen will run a marathon this year

Dylet ti fynd i'r gwely
You should go to bed

Preterite verbs and short-form verbs

Preterite verbs in English usually end in *-ed* if they are regular. This is the past tense that doesn't use the verb *have* (i.e. the perfect tense, see above). It's sometimes referred to as the 'simple past'.

Cerddais i ar hyd yr afon
I walked along the river

In Welsh, the **berfau cryno** (*short-form verbs*) are conjugated for the corresponding person, which means the pronouns can be dropped from formal sentences.

Cerddaist (ti) i'r dref
You walked to town

Cerddodd (hi) i fyny'r mynydd
She walked up the mountain

Verbal-nouns

What is a verbal-noun you ask? It's tricky. I'm never sure I understand fully myself. Verbal-nouns are words which could be thought of as nouns or as verbs depending on the context in which they appear. It can be difficult to translate these into English sometimes. You might have to suspend your English for a bit for the first sentence below (which is in the passive voice):

Mae'r castell wedi'i ddinistrio
The castle has been destroyed (literally: *The castle is after its destroying*)

Hyfryd yw canu adar mân
[The] small birds' singing is lovely

The following sentence contains a very common error for learners to make. Here **i** has been added to make an English-style infinitive (see above) *to sing*:

*Gofynna iddo fe i ganu!
Ask him to sing!

Here someone's tried to directly translate an English sentence into Welsh. But there isn't really an infinitive (i.e. *to sing*) here at all. It's actually a verbal-noun. The sentence should be:

Gofynna iddo fe ganu!
Ask him to sing!

The verbal-noun **canu** is the direct object (see previous section on objects) of the verb **gofynna**. Perhaps we need a rule to remember here. If the verbal-noun is a subject or an object of a verb (i.e. when it's really acting like a noun), then we don't use the preposition **i**. But if the verbal-noun is used like an adverb to convey some kind of idea involving purpose (i.e. "in order to") then we do stick **i** in front of it. Here are two sentences demonstrating this difference:

Dyweda iddyn nhw orffen y gwaith nawr
Tell them to finish the work now

Rhoddais i gyfle iddyn nhw i siarad
I gave them chance to speak

That's probably clear as mud...! Don't worry about these verbal-nouns. They're really things you need a lot of exposure to in order to grasp because there isn't an English equivalent you can grab onto for comparison. Keep reading in Welsh, keep listening to Welsh as much as possible and eventually these annoying verbal-nouns will be firmly under your control.

Answers: Be' sy'n bod?

The mutations

Soft mutations

1. Roedd **cath** mawr ar y bwrdd (*There was a big cat on the table*)
    a. **f**awr
2. Aeth e **i** Caerfyrddin (*He went to Carmarthen*)
    a. **G**aerfyrddin
3. Mae **hen** dyn yn byw drws nesaf (*An old man lives next door*)
    a. **dd**yn
4. Roedd **dau** ci gyda nhw (*They had two dogs*)
    a. **g**i
5. Siwan yw enw **ei** mam e (*His mum's name is Siwan*)
    a. **f**am
6. Gwelodd **hi** bachgen ar y to (*She saw a boy on the roof*)
    a. **f**achgen

Nasal mutations

1. Dw i'n byw yn Ngaerdydd [Caerdydd]
    a. y**ng Ng**haerdydd
2. Jon yw enw fy martner [partner]
    a. fy **mh**arter
3. Caeth hi swydd yn Mhorth [Borth]
    a. y**m M**orth
4. Mae fy nghesg wrth ymyl y ffenestr [desg]
    a. fy **n**esg
5. Mae ei theulu'n byw yn Mhrefdraeth [Trefdraeth]
    a. y**n Nh**refdraeth
6. Mae'r gath yn gorwedd ar fy nghwely [gwely]
    a. fy **ng**wely

Aspirate mutations

1. Dyw ei dad ddim yn gwybod am hyn (*Her dad doesn't know about this*)
    a. dad > tad > **th**ad
2. Mae tri gi yn yr ardd (*There are three dogs in the garden*)
    a. gi > ci > **ch**i
3. Gwen ei enw ei bartner (*Gwen is her partner's name*)
    a. bartner > partner > **ph**artner
4. Coffi a de (*coffee and tea*)
    a. de > te > **th**e
5. Mae ei dractor wedi torri i lawr (*Her tractor's broken down*)
    a. dractor > tractor > **th**ractor
6. Chwe bunt! (*Six pounds!*)
    a. bunt > punt > **ph**unt

Yes/No

Incorrect responses are given in brackets and correct responses in bold.

1. Dych chi'n byw yn Llundain? > (ie) **ydw**
2. Ydyn nhw'n priodi'r flwyddyn nesaf? > (ydy) **ydyn**
3. Oes brawd neu chwaer gyda hi? > (nac ydw) **nac oes**
4. O'dd amser gyda chi ymweld â'r Mont-St-Michel? > (oes) **oedd**
5. Fyddwn ni'n mynd draw i'w gweld hi ddydd Mawrth? > (bydd) **byddwn**
6. Hi oedd yn y parti? > (oedd) **ie**
7. Fydd e eisiau copi o'r llyfr newydd? > (na fyddi) **bydd**
8. Wnei di baned o de i fi? > (nage) **na wnaf**
9. Fyddet ti'n hapus gyda'r syniad? > (byddaf) b**yddwn**
10. Fyddai hi eisiau symud i Ddenmarc? > (na fydd) **byddai**
11. Ga i edrych? > (wyt) **cei**
12. Awures enwog yw hi? > (nac ydy) **nag**
13. Gawn ni fwy o gawl? > (na chei) **na chewch**
14. Wnewch chi ysgrifennu'r cost yma? > (ydw) **gwnaf**
15. Yn Llundain maen nhw'n byw? > (ydyn) **ie**
16. O'dd Jon yn y parti? > (nac oes) **nac oedd**

The verb *to be*

1. Dw **i'n** ddim yn mynd (*I'm not going*)

    a. Dw **i** ddim yn mynd

2. **B**ydd e ddim yn hapus (*He won't be happy*)

    a. **F**ydd e ddim yn hapus

3. **Ro't** chi'n arfer byw yn y Ffindir (*You used to live in Finland*)

    a. **Ro'ch** chi'n arfer byw yn y Ffindir

4. **Mae** hi ddim wedi ennill (*She hasn't won*)

    a. **Dyw** hi ddim wedi ennill

5. **Fydd** y coleg ar gau (*The college will be closed*)

    a. **Bydd** y coleg ar gau

6. Dwyt ti**'n** gwybod (*You don't know*)

    a. Dwyt ti **ddim yn** gwybod

7. Fyddan nhw **dim** yn gallu eich helpu (*They won't be able to help you*)

    a. Fyddan nhw **ddim** yn gallu eich helpu

8. Dyw e**'n** gallu chwarae'r delyn (*He can't play the harp*)

    a. Dyw e **ddim yn** gallu chwarae'r delyn

9. **Roedden** y plant ar wyliau (*The children were on holiday*)

    a. **Roedd** y plant ar wyliau

10. Dw i **dim** yn gweld y pwynt (*I can't see the point*)

    a. Dw i **ddim** yn gweld y pwynt

Gair o ddiolch

Diolch to my students at London's City Literary Institute whose insightful questions and grammatical frustrations gave me the idea for this book. I'm also grateful to my tutees in London and further afield for their valuable feedback on certain sections of the book. **Diolch o galon** to Lucy Culshaw for the fantastic cover illustration.

A diolch i chi for picking up this book! **Pob lwc gyda'r dysgu- daliwch ati!**

Jack Pulman-Slater, Llundain 2019

Printed in Great Britain
by Amazon